THE WARMTH MEDITATION

The early Christian physicians Cosmas and Damian,
Essen Cathedral, Church of Münster, Germany
(photograph © by Sophia van Dijk)

THE WARMTH MEDITATION

A Path to the Good
in the Service of Healing

Peter Selg

SteinerBooks | 2016

SteinerBooks
An imprint of Anthropsophic Press, Inc.
610 Main St., Great Barrington, MA 01230
www.steinerbooks.org

 This book was originally published in German as *Die «Wärme-Meditation»: Geschichtlicher Hintergrund und ideelle Beziehungen* (Verlag am Goetheanum, Dornach, Switzerland, 2005; 2nd edition 2013).

Translated by Rory Bradley
Cover image: Blackboard drawing
from Rudolf Steiner's lecture course
The Cycle of the Year as a Breathing Process of the Earth,
lecture of March 31, 1923
(Anthroposophic Press, 1984)
Design by Jens Jensen

Library of Congress Control Number: 2016953914

ISBN: 978-1-62148-162-1 (paperback)
ISBN: 978-1-62148-163-8 (ebook)

Printed in the United States of America

Contents

Preface to the Second German Edition by Michaela Glöckler vii

Foreword xiii

I Historical Connections 1

II Spiritual Connections 29

Appendix 53

Notes 59

Preface to the Second German Edition

Peter Selg remarks in his foreword to this text that it will be essential "in the days to come" (and perhaps even more then than now) to be able to hold in one's consciousness the unusually solemn signature of the historical and spiritual/ideational (*ideellen*) circumstances under which the "Warmth Meditation" came to be. How can one accomplish this? Many years have already passed since the first printing of the meditation in 1999.

Rudolf Steiner gave the Warmth Meditation to Helene von Grunelius in 1924 so that she might then share it with a group of young doctors and medical students in preparation for working together in a course with Rudolf Steiner. With this began a process of passing the meditation along personally to doctors and medical students who felt that anthroposophical medicine was a matter that lay close to their hearts.

This continued until 1999. The meditation was personally passed on from doctor to doctor, colleague to colleague, never leaving the circles of those who worked with it actively. It was no different for me at the end of my medical studies. In conversation with an experienced doctor, it came about that she passed the Warmth Meditation on to me for my inner medical work, connecting it with several beautiful remarks about the Christian approach to anthroposophical medicine, the secrets of Mercury, and the Mystery of Raphael. I have never encountered the Warmth Meditation except in an atmosphere of brotherly friendship and generous love. Even if—as Peter Selg indicates in this text—there were some serious things happening among the so-called young doctors connected with Rudolf Steiner when they received this meditation, its substance is completely at home in a sphere that brings healing to those suffering from illness or difficult social conditions. It brings to the doctor additional sources of healing etheric energy.

Whenever a meditation such as this is published widely, thereby leaving the circles for which it was intended, it not only raises a question about the legitimacy of this course of action but also, and perhaps more important, raises a question about how one can work appropriately with it under these new circumstances. Peter Selg has already spoken about the legitimacy of this publication. I would simply like to add that it is also self-evident to me that, after being kept in secret for a certain period of time, a meditation that is so helpful to doctors and therapists should be allowed to find its way through the printed word to those awaiting it and who need it.

The current understanding of the practice and preservation of the Warmth Meditation in the circles of the anthroposophical medical movement is as follows: We assume, as we always have, that this meditation was given to doctors for their inner work and the support of their therapeutic capacities. Yet this crucial exercise could also be helpful for other professions that engage with therapeutic work. Is it possible to satisfy both? Dr. Karl König, the founder of the Camphill movement, offers a wonderful example of how it can. He gave the meditation to his colleagues, including those who were not doctors, and this promoted a spiritual approach to their collaboration in the service of those in need. He also found ways of passing on the meditation that elevated it above everyday routine, lending a celebratory and special character to the process. It is recommended that when members of a therapy profession who are not doctors want to work with this meditation, they talk about it first with an anthroposophical doctor, so that as this meditation moves out of doctors' circles, it can be accompanied by explanations and a kind of conscious handing-over. In any case, doctors still give it to their colleagues as needed, as has always been the case, and they will also mention Peter Selg's publication of it.

But what about those who do not belong to groups of either therapists or doctors? Here it is a question of spiritual tact—whether they want to devote themselves to the underlying intention of the work or, through the study of this text, they will be satisfied with knowledge of such a task. Precisely in a time such as ours, when everything is being made available publicly, people must learn to decide for themselves whether things are suited to their temperament or work. It can also be the case (as it is here) that questions and provocations arise in connection with what Peter Selg has described that lead to new perspectives on the esoteric foundation of one's own work in life.

Rudolf Steiner says of the Warmth Meditation that it can provide doctors access to the working of the etheric Christ. But the question of such access is *the* question that every human being hopes to grasp through a life of worship, and for that there are many possible paths, many guiding words and thoughts.

A heartfelt wish accompanies this book: that the unconquerable will to goodness, which speaks out of the Warmth Meditation, reproduced and described here, may have an awakening effect on all those who pick up this little volume.

Michaela Glöckler, October 2013
Medical Section of the Goetheanum

Foreword

On September 20, 2004—the anniversary of the groundbreaking of the first Goetheanum—at the annual conference of the Medical Section of the Goetheanum, I offered an evening lecture, at the request of Michaela Glöckler, on the historical conditions and the spiritual surroundings of the central medical meditation that Helene von Grunelius received from Rudolf Steiner in 1923 and that has been maintained and practiced by countless individuals during the past eight decades—becoming for many the existential core of their therapeutic practice and perspective. The edited manuscript of my remarks is printed in the following pages.

If one is to take up what is found here, several things should be kept in mind, particularly the *situation* and the *intention* of the description reproduced here in print. The people who come together in the middle of

September each year at the Goetheanum are engaged in therapeutic work and tasks in many different countries all over the world, often under very challenging circumstances. They undertake long journeys to come to the annual conference of the Medical Section—and they do so in order to engage with the collected experiences of others working with anthroposophical medicine and thereby gain social orientation, and in order to maintain a connection between their own individual work and the central stream of anthroposophical science, if not with the very Being *Anthroposophia*. Every contribution to this gathering must take account of these conditions—one can count not only on the seriousness of consciousnesses dedicated to therapeutic work, but also on the underlying will forces of such people who have made a connection with Anthroposophy and with the kind of healing that it enables in the whole destiny of their lives.

When the assignment was given to shed some light on the historical and spiritual conditions of the so-called Warmth Meditation, it was with the understanding that the audience not only would be generally inclined to "take interest" in the conditions that would be described, but would also be struck and moved by it both inwardly and in their daily work. A great deal in the cited words, and in the biographies of the doctors who were around Rudolf Steiner and were connected with the events of 1923/1924, would resonate with what lived in the hearts of those who were present at the conference, as well as in their personal connections with those who had passed on—with relatives, friends, and sponsors. The level of attention this created made possible an intensity of the spoken and heard word that can no longer be found in this printed, and thus abstracted (removed from the life process) reproduction—an intensity that is connected with the unmistakable spiritual profile of the Goetheanum and that exhibits a specific dimension of destiny.

But at the same time, the specific conditions in which the lecture of September 20, 2004, was presented and received played out within the context of a historical moment that lent a particular inflection to its primary focus (which, on the surface, was specifically oriented toward medicine)—indeed, a kind of intensification, and one that was certainly rooted in its spiritual origins—that caused it to spread out into the general reality of civilization. When one speaks three years after 9/11 in the Dornach Goetheanum about a therapeutic meditation that, in its first, preparatory section, begins with the question "How do I find the Good?" there can be little doubt that countless events from the recent past have become part of the thematic (even if not expressly)—global, world-historical events, with as yet unforeseeable consequences for the future of civilization on earth, involving figures who were misled into fundamentalist sacrifices for the supposed "Good" as well as those who responded with a self-destructive answer, believing themselves capable of deciding between "Good" and "Evil" and of ordering the world anew.

In a less politically visible way, but in a way that is connected with the inmost substance of the topic, as well as its therapeutic effects, the old European question of the being and the becoming of the Good also becomes part of the thematic—the theme and content of the central esoteric lectures Plato gave to the inner circle of his Academy (*Peri Agathon*, "On the Good"[1]), after which came the turn of the eras and the pioneering words of Christ recorded in the Gospel of Luke: "Why do you call me good? No one is good except God alone" (18:19).[2] In this Christological formulation—one of the most important guiding lights in the historical formation of Anthroposophy—the opening lines of the mantra discussed at the Dornach Goetheanum describe the path to finding the *Good* as the precondition for all sacred striving on behalf of the human being in the world; the means of finding the divine Good, whose ontological Being cannot be understood as an essential attribute of the individual (as a category to be judged morally), despite all current political tendencies to do so. Rather, the Good is connected with the individual's intentional will to service-oriented activity ("*I can physically realize the Good*")—the will to a service-oriented, therapeutic work in which the individual's ongoing transformation, his or her work and life impulses can be realized with a complete and constant orientation toward the future: "All will be good,/That we/root in our hearts,/That we/guide with our heads,/With will."[3]

The so-called Warmth Meditation belongs to the spiritual center of anthroposophical medicine and, in certain and specific ways, to the Christmas events at the turn of the years 1923 to 1924, the spiritual "*World—Turning of the Eras—Beginning.*" An examination of the special and unusually serious signature of the historical and ideological circumstances under which it was first formulated by Rudolf Steiner for Helene von Grunelius is the narrow topic of the aforementioned lecture presentation. It is more essential than ever that this signature (independent from the meditative experiences and accounts of the particular doctors or therapists) continue to be held in consciousness in the future—the time following the publication (first in 1999) and subsequent distribution of a mantra that in the first years and decades of its use lived in the circle of trust of only a narrow group of people, guarded and protected there carefully and with respectful reverence and with educated historical consciousness.

As never before, but with thorough inner consistency, these processes are now placed freely at the disposal of the individual, opening up certain possibilities, but also false paths and grave uncertainty. Meditative exercises and mantric formulas are—despite their often evident and recognizable beauty—not poems; they can take hold in the lives of individuals in ways that are consistently uplifting and promoting, but they can also make it possible, through false application, to direct forces in the wrong direction and are thus susceptible, through lack of knowledge and also recklessness, to "desecration," which Rudolf Steiner would sometimes stress. In regard to the Warmth Meditation, a situation arose, for example, in which the old traditions, the concrete connotations, and the very consciously managed considerations of passing on the meditation were completely disregarded—an irreversible situation that brought about greater social openness and expansion, but also brought with it the danger of spiritual leveling and the decline of esoteric effectiveness.

To assess it now in light of a positive therapeutic turn of events, to compile and make public the spiritual physiognomy of the mantra by referring to the collected documents of the Ita Wegman Archive and to other studies (at least in outline form), can possibly have a helpful if not methodologically path-finding significance. It might allow for a deep, spiritual interiorization of the experiences and working conditions of Rudolf Steiner's lifetime as the knowledge required for present and future exercises and tasks. The following pages, dedicated in gratitude to Ita Wegman, will address these connections.

Peter Selg

The Warmth Meditation

Preparation: How do I find the Good?

1. Can I think the Good?

   I cannot think the Good.
   Thinking is brought about by my ether body.
   My ether body works in the fluidity of my body.
   So I do not find the Good in the fluidity of the body.

2. Can I feel the Good?

   I can certainly feel the Good, but it is not there
   through me if I only feel it.
   Feeling is brought about by my astral body.
   My astral body works in the air element
   of my body.
   So I do not find the Good that exists through me
   in the air element of the body.

3. Can I will the Good?

   I can will the Good.
   Willing is brought about by my "I".
   My "I" works in the warmth ether of my body.
   So I can realize the Good physically in the warmth.

Vorbereitung: Wie finde ich das Gute?

1. Kann ich das Gute denken?

Ich kann das Gute nicht denken.
Denken versorgt mein Ätherleib.
Mein Ätherleib wirkt in der Flüssigkeit meines Leibes.
Also in der Flüssigkeit des Leibes finde ich das Gute nicht.

2. Kann ich das Gut e fühlen?

Ich kann das Gute zwar fühlen; aber es ist durch mich nicht da, wen nich es nur fühle.
Fühlen versorgt mein astralischer Leib.
Mein astralischer Leib wirkt in dem Luftförmigen meines Leibes.
Also in dem Luftförmigen des Leibes finde ich das durch mich existierende Gute nicht.

3. Kann ich das Gute wollen?

Ich kann das Gute wollen.
Wollen versorgt mein Ich.
Mein Ich wirkt in dem Wärmeäther meines Leibes.
Also in der Wärme kann ich das Gute physisch verwirklichen.

[Meditation]: I feel my humanity in my warmth.

1. I feel light in my warmth.

   (Take care that this sensation of light emerges in the region where the physical heart is.)

2. I feel the substance of the world resonating in my warmth.

   (Take care that the unusual sound-sensation, spreading out into the whole body, goes from the lower body to the head.)

3. I feel in my head the world-life moving in my warmth.

   (Take care that the unusual sensation of life spreads from the head to the whole body.)[4]

Ich fühle meine Menschheit in meiner Wärme.

1. Ich fühle Licht in meiner Wärme.

(Achtgeben, dass diese Lichtempfindung auftritt in der Gegend, wo das physische Herz ist)

2. Ich fühle tönend die Weltsubstanz in meiner Wärme.

(Achtgeben, dass die eigentümliche Ton-Empfindung vom Unterleib nach dem Kopfe, aber mit Ausbreitung im ganzen Leibe geht.)

3. Ich fühle in meinem Kopfe sich regend das Weltenleben in meiner Wärme.

(Achtgeben, dass die eigentümliche Lebensempfindung vom Kopfe nach dem ganzen Körper sich verbreitet)

I

Historical Connections

Then he [Rudolf Steiner] gave her [Ita Wegman] the Warmth Meditation and said that she was allowed to give it to all future participants. He wanted to give it to Dr. Wegman himself. It is a chain-meditation, not a circle-meditation. Then he described it as the way for medical practitioners to behold the etheric Christ.

— Madeleine van Deventer[5]

Rudolf Steiner wrote the text of the Warmth Meditation on two sheets of A4 paper in neat handwriting and without revisions or corrections, complete with two small, sketch-like drawings.[6]

When exactly he wrote this down and what context surrounded it is not known in detail. Everything that has been known about it until now comes from the accounts of Doctor Madeleine van Deventer (1899–1983), the colleague of Ita Wegman and long-standing director of the Arlesheim clinic,[7] who at the very end of her life sought to describe the historical development of the anthroposophical medical movement in a written record ("The anthroposophical medical movement in the various stages of its development"[8]). From December 1925—when she came to the Clinical Therapeutic Institute in Arlesheim—van Deventer was deeply involved with everything that Ita Wegman did, and from March 1920 she had also already participated in numerous lectures given in Dornach by Rudolf Steiner to doctors, most notably the courses on the inner and outer organism for medical students and young doctors that Rudolf Steiner was finally able to give in January and April 1924, which she dutifully attended with her friend Helene von Frunelius (1897–1936).[9] In the second chapter of her memoirs, which first appeared in 1982 and is the centerpiece of her accounts, van Deventer addressed the developments that accompanied these courses, describing the striving and dissatisfaction of the young, anthroposophically oriented students: their discontent with the training situation at universities and their wish for further indications from Rudolf Steiner that went beyond the medical remarks he had made thus far and that would describe the moral path of the future doctor. Madeleine van Deventer described the various conditions under which the student initiative slowly developed around Helene von Grunelius, involving countless individual conversations and encounters between the doctor, who died so young, and Rudolf Steiner—for example, in the late fall of 1923, just a few months before the eventual start of the course. Helene von Grunelius, according to van Deventer, was at the time experiencing a situation of personal uncertainty about Steiner's indications about methods of studying—in a preparatory talk delivered to the medical students (including young assistant doctors), he had advised them to train themselves to compare the diagnostic methods of natural science and spiritual science and to write down their results in a notebook.[10] Thereafter, she went to see Rudolf Steiner in Dornach and received extensive helpful exercises for herself and her friends:

> Helene complained that it was impossible for her to follow the advice about the "notebook," because you never know whether the things you write on the right [the spiritual-scientific] side are correct. Rudolf Steiner answered: *"that does not matter, you will correct yourself over time. And in any case, you can send your notebooks to me. But if you want to feel more 'certainty,' I can give you a meditation."* Then he gave her the Warmth Meditation and said that she was allowed to give it to all future participants. He wanted to give it to Dr. Wegman himself.
>
> It is a chain-meditation, not a circle-meditation. Then he described it as the way for medical practitioners to behold the etheric Christ.[11]

When Madeleine van Deventer wrote down these sentences in 1982, she was eighty-three years old. Almost six decades had passed since this conversation had taken place in Rudolf Steiner's atelier in Dornach. Madeleine van Deventer did not have any written record from this period, which she spent not in Dornach or

Arlesheim, but rather studying in Dutch Utrecht—but the central content of the occurrence surrounding the Warmth Meditation was fully and clearly present for her: *"Then he described it as the way for medical practitioners to behold the etheric Christ."*

There is some reason to believe that Madeleine van Deventer's recollections of the moment when the Warmth Meditation was given to Helene von Grunelius differ in regard to the timing (not, however, the content[12]) of the events in that period.[13] The documents from the Ita Wegman Archive make the dating of when Rudolf Steiner wrote down the mantra, and indirectly when he gave it to Ita Wegman ("He wanted to give it to Dr. Wegman himself"), seem questionable at best—not least because von Grunelius herself, in a letter to Ita Wegman from December 1926 (just a little more than three years after she had received the mantra), spoke decisively about the Warmth Meditation, "which we received in *spring 1923*."[14]

Various other circumstances indicate that the meditation was given in the middle of March 1923, during a "very significant conversation for our medical work with the Dr." that Helene von Grunelius had with Rudolf Steiner, which she reported on in a letter written just fourteen days later to her sister Marie Wundt (born

Grunelius).[15] That spring and early summer, 1923, just a few months after the shocking fire that burned down the first Goetheanum, Helene von Grunelius continued on the basis of directives received from Rudolf Steiner, participating quite intensively in the development and furthering of the Free Anthroposophical Society, for which Steiner had written a special "Memorandum" on March 11.[16] This time was fueled inwardly by the foundational lectures delivered in Dornach during the second week of June, in which Steiner called for "self-reflection" on the part of anthroposophists in a manner far more clear than ever before.[17]

In the spirit of these lectures—and with formulations that belong together with the language of the Christmastime events and, in a certain sense, signify true "anticipation" in the soul of a young person destined for Michaelic work—Helene von Grunelius issued a call to anthroposophically oriented medical students, speaking about the fact that future medical work has a "purpose-driven, clear path" to travel and that it must be based "in the heart, the center of Anthroposophy," rather than in reductive intellectual powers. Only then can the medical path, and with it the establishment of the anthroposophical medical movement, receive the "proper impetus," and lead to a spiritually founded moral code of medical activity. ("Then we will be able to see and show how the soul-spiritual works its way into the physical, giving it form and differentiation, but also how this physical element in people can be retransformed into the soul-spiritual through the activity of moral impulses in the warm heart forces of the human being."[18]) Countless perspectives that Rudolf Steiner has already opened up for Helene von Grunelius and her friends played an essential role in these formulations—but von Grunelius herself took conscious, willing responsibility for it, co-signing the appeal with medical students Manfred von Kries and Henk van Deventer. Henk van Deventer, the brother of Madeleine van Deventer, whom Helene von Grunelius had gotten to know in March 1923 in Dornach and who had long been preoccupied with the question of a medical student association, but who would die just three years later in the summer of 1926, described this newsletter in writing to his sister at the end of August as "Helene's appeal." Henk van Deventer was uncertain at this point whether the student assembly described at the end of the letter could perhaps be sensibly incorporated into the context of a course with Rudolf Steiner. ("If you would like to work with us in this spirit, we would ask you to contact us soon, that we might begin our work together as soon as possible, and that an assembly could take place sometime in the fall or during the holiday break."[19]) For his part, Rudolf Steiner instead makes a case for an intensification of the meditative work that had already begun in a smaller circle. In light of what he writes in this letter, there is much to indicate that Helene von Grunelius had already passed on the Warmth Meditation in the spring to him and a few other friends connected with the preparation of the future medical work; there is also much to indicate that a small medical-esoteric meditation group had already begun in secret among the young students around Easter of 1923. Henk wrote something to this effect (and in the style of his generation) on August 21, 1923, to Madeleine van Deventer:

> How would it be if we were able to expand the meditation circle? I would not expect much from a course if the appeal was made just to anthroposophical medical practitioners. If people have not yet been moved, then they are nothing more than "Sunday anthroposophists." In other words: an infinite enrichment of life through anth., but...to really connect with the field, to take it up in the will? No, not that! Of course they grumble, because Herr Dr. is withholding the course. They hear their own limitations in everything.

> Perhaps I misjudge them, and the many anthroposophical medical practitioners are just waiting for their wake-up call. Then a general appeal to the anthroposophists would indeed be good. But then you have to really vet the people who respond.[20]

We do not yet know which people belonged at this time to the medical "meditation circle" to which Henk van Deventer refers, but apart from him and Helene von Grunelius, it probably included his wife Erna (nee Wolfram), who practiced therapeutic eurythmy, and Madeleine van Deventer. At the end of October 1923, Helene von Grunelius asked Rudolf Steiner in Dornach for personal permission to pass along the meditation exercise to others. ("On behalf of the others, I asked the Doctor about Bockholt and Groth."[21]) Rudolf Steiner not only agreed to this request, but was surprised that Margarethe Bockholt, the young Arlesheim doctor and therapeutic eurythmist whom he held in high regard, had not already received the meditation by that point.

~

When Helene von Grunelius spent a week in Dornach and Arlesheim at the end of October 1923 in order to speak with Rudolf Steiner about the details of the course that she continued to fight for and prepare for (though Henk van Deventer had voted against it)—including when exactly it would happen, who would be invited to participate, and how to handle the older anthroposophical doctors—the situation in the anthroposophical medical movement had fundamentally changed, at least in regard to the spiritual content of the work being done.

Two months before, Ita Wegman had come to Rudolf Steiner with questions about a future Mystery Medicine. Wegman's questions had, along with her karmic insights, established the preconditions that allowed Rudolf Steiner not only to begin significant lectures on the essence of both the old and new Mysteries, and on the Christmas Conference and the reformulation of the Anthroposophical Society, but also to begin his medical-esoteric collaboration with Ita Wegman.[22] That Rudolf Steiner would have felt more or less obligated, in the spring of 1923, to pass on a meditation developed for the medical students around Helene von Grunelius ("He wanted to give it to Dr. Wegman himself") is downright improbable. By the end of 1923, on the other hand, in connection with the Christmas Conference, responsibility for the medical work was handed over to Ita Wegman, with whom Rudolf Steiner intended to lead the newly founded Medical Section.

During the course for Helene von Grunelius's group (as well as several other doctors whom Rudolf Steiner had specially invited), which actually began on January 2, 1924, he said, "You must have complete trust in how the medical division of the Goetheanum will be led by me together with Frau Dr. Wegman."[23]

Details about how the course went—its conditions, perspectives and difficulties—are reported in the biographical monograph about Helene von Grunelius;[24] the content of the course and its relationship to the Christmas Conference is related in a later work.[25] In regard to the Warmth Meditation itself, it is of considerable historical import that from January 1924 on, Rudolf Steiner placed it fully in the hands of Ita Wegman, which is to say that he made it the spiritual responsibility of the leader of the Medical Section of the Goetheanum. In response to a question (no longer extant) from one of the course participants about the continuing path of medical study and the possibility of receiving the Warmth Meditation, Rudolf Steiner (together with Ita Wegman) responded on March 11 in writing:

> Regarding a question about the difficulties facing the prospective doctor both in the study of academic medicine and also in the medical courses

> of the anthroposophical movement, we can only respond that we are striving, through the distribution of these newsletters, to resolve these difficulties in time. Dr. Wegman is prepared to give the supplemental meditation to those who have need of it.[6]

At the time of this first (and only) "newsletter," Helene von Grunelius did not yet understand that this referred to the Warmth Meditation and that the way it would be passed on in the future had been established—she wrote to Madeleine van Deventer on March 30, 1924 (exactly a year before Rudolf Steiner's death), asking which "supplemental" meditation was being referred to in this newsletter.[27]

~

But at the same time, after the course in January and the following one at Easter, the Warmth Meditation continued to have the same central significance for Helene von Grunelius that it had from the start—she took it seriously and resolutely. In a manner unlike any of the others in the group, Grunelius experienced Rudolf Steiner's dissatisfaction with the young audience, with the lack of resolve he saw in the group, with the insufficient will orientation toward the medical realization of Anthroposophy following the Christmas Conference, in particular with the insufficient formation by the group of a spiritual foundation, especially as regards the developing social form and work of the Medical Section ("Herr Dr. is extremely dissatisfied with us. He says that we do not know what we want; we have no backbone, etc. Who among us would not feel similarly dissatisfied with us!"[28]).

Most of the young medical practitioners had been pleased and uplifted by Rudolf Steiner's lectures, evidently without being able to truly experience the social-spiritual prompts they contained. By August 1924 at the latest, Grunelius (along with several other course participants[29]) realized the extent to which everyone was lagging behind and wrote to her friends about the absolute necessity of developing now, in the immediate future, a real certainty and a community of will—indeed, a "codified will to action"—while there was still time. In the context of these letters, which Grunelius wrote immediately after the end of her medical studies and at a time when she was starting to develop signs of illness, and also very clearly with a pressing premonition of the brief time left in Rudolf Steiner's life, her contact with the Warmth Meditation played a small but important role. On August 17, she wrote about it to Madeleine van Deventer:

> Frau Dr. Wegman has now given our meditation to Buettner, Ungar, Kahnert and Foerstner. I do not know whether she has also given it to others in the meantime. The whole matter of this meditation is a dark one. Our movement would not be in such poor condition if we had not failed so utterly on this point—namely the meditation group, which was to have been the heart of the medical movement. And now this heart can *only* be formed by people who have this meditation (those who have the inner sense of needing this meditation can receive it from Frau Dr. Wegman).[30]

From Grunelius's writings, one thing among many that becomes clear is that Ita Wegman told Helene von Grunelius about each time that she passed on the meditation, either directly or through Margarethe Bockholt,[31] which means that she still took on the original responsibility for contact with the mantra and took it absolutely seriously. Helene von Grunelius herself had an intense conversation with Rudolf Steiner at the end of July or beginning of August (after his return from Arnheim and before his departure for Torquay) in which they discussed not only the above-mentioned dissatisfaction with the individual and social proceedings in the group of young medical students, but also in which Grunelius asked Rudolf Steiner quite openly for further assistance with the Warmth Meditation. Addressing that briefly and outlining her own, most recent efforts, Helene von Grunelius wrote to Margarethe Bockholt, just four days after her letter to Madeleine van Deventer:

> Herr Dr. said to me recently: you must try to live more fully into the essence of this meditation, to connect yourself more strongly with it, and then what you seek will come (he said something along those lines).
>
> I was not at all clear about how I was to do that. In my first days here I mostly read that book by Wachsmuth, which is truly wonderful and illuminated my thoughts. Apart from that, I read our medical course from Easter, but that only made me more doubtful. In the first few days I felt worse from day to day, until I actually got to the point of feeling sick. My temperature rose somewhat, and then I stayed completely in bed for two days. Once I started to feel a little better, I lay on a sofa on the balcony or, when it was too cold outside, in the room. I then read the three lectures from December 1920, which are actually quite connected with the meditation. At first, I felt like nothing made sense, until suddenly, in the morning of the day before yesterday, when I was reading the lecture cycle on the Gospel of Luke again,

the lights came on for me. Since then, I have also felt almost completely healthy!

I believe that really diving into the essence of this meditation can give us the proper karmic will. I believe that, at least for those who have this meditation, it is *the* path to bringing forth a karmic will and will to action from within. In this, I agree with you completely, that our karmic will must be there first in order to undertake the new formation of an esoteric circle, if it is to be a circle that really leads and takes initiative.[32]

Despite these efforts on the part of Helene von Grunelius and her friends, the intended formation of an esoteric circle for anthroposophical medicine did not ultimately take shape in the larger community sphere of young medical practitioners (which had, over the course of a long period of time, continued to grow, despite many difficulties), nor did it build upon the connective foundation of the Warmth Meditation—even though all of the (seven, later nine) members of the "esoteric core,"[33] which was endorsed by Rudolf Steiner and mentioned for the first time on September 18, were to be among the audience of the courses in January and at Easter. The social events from September 1924 that preceded the reduced "core formation" are not known in detail, nor could they be established from any documentary evidence, before now.[34] The utterly serious words from Grunelius's letter, however, serve as a testament to the accuracy of her premonitions about the organism that finally came into being. The members of this spiritual-therapeutic coalition ultimately could not develop a strong "karma will," and they failed as the esoteric core of the Medical Section sometime before March 30, 1925.[35] In any case, Ita Wegman considered the efforts of this organism (despite the great and noble motivations of the individuals involved) unsuccessful in hindsight, and wrote a significant (and thought-provoking) memorial note about it in 1936:

> We made...a very small beginning. The curative principles of the various Mysteries, brought together in one school. Michael and Raphael, working together!
>
> Sadly it was not to be; you could clearly feel the earth resisting. The earth and human beings did not want such a tremendous spirituality. Dr. Steiner then left this earthly work, of his own will; his illness was only a Maya. And human beings were left, alone...

~

Despite this—or rather, with an awareness of the greater responsibility that was laid upon them because of it—countless people around Helene von Grunelius and Ita Wegman continued to work following Rudolf Steiner's death on the content of the course for young medical practitioners, the mantras from January and April 1924, and the Warmth Meditation, in particular. Until her death in 1943, Ita Wegman retained personal responsibility for the circulation and spread of this spiritual–mantric substance of anthroposophical medicine.

Wegman was, and remained for Helen von Grunelius, the person with the final say, because Rudolf Steiner had entrusted her with this task and considered her capable of it. When Grunelius, at the end of December 1926, wanted to pass on the lecture notes and mantric exercises (among them the meditation "that we received in the spring of 1923 [on the 'good']") to her colleague Anna Iduna Zehnter, she asked Wegman for her consent, which she immediately received. Ita Wegman, for her part, considered it important that the spread of the courses for young medical practitioners be handled in a very particular way, and she usually gave the lecture transcripts to medical colleagues and students only on the condition that the person asking for them was ready and able to work through the course with one of the original participants. Everything exclusive or elitist was as foreign to Ita Wegman as the concept of "spiritual succession" or "esoteric claims to power";[36] but independent of all that, she was determined to maintain a sense of personal connection and responsibility, and to protect the spiritual characteristics of the original initiatives that surrounded Helene von Grunelius. ("Indeed, the esoteric survives inasmuch as it remains within the circle to which it was entrusted."[37] [Rudolf Steiner]) When the anthroposophical doctor Johannes Kroker, who was active in Breslau and later in Pilgramshain (among other places), wrote to her regarding the possibility of obtaining the January and Easter courses, as well as the Pastoral Medicine course from September 1924, Wegman answered him with a somewhat lengthy explanation that demonstrates her basic understanding of the mantric-social spirit of the courses for young medical practitioners; she writes:

Arlesheim, June 8, 1927
Dear Herr Dr. Kroker!

I have received your letter, in which you asked about the medical courses for young doctors that were held at Christmas and Easter, as well as the Pastoral Medicine course. As soon as you are taken into the First Class, which you are also asking about currently, you may have the Pastoral Medicine course. As regards the Christmas and Easter courses for young doctors—there is a group of young people who received meditations during both of these courses, and as such (according to Dr. Steiner's own words), this is a group who connected with one another through these meditations in order to take those meditations deeper into themselves and to understand them. As such, I must first ask you, before you can obtain these courses, whether you want to belong to this group of people; the people who are part of it must then of course also attempt to live in accord with another, because otherwise the meditations will not have their intended effects. Perhaps it would be good, dear Herr Dr. Kroker, if you were to come sometime to Dornach, that we might be able to speak about these matters in more detail with one another, and in regard to taking part in the class as well. I am pleased that you are called to this beautiful work.

With kindest regards,
Dr. I. Wegman[38]

According to this, Rudolf Steiner and Ita Wegman considered the doctors and medical students around Helene von Grunelius a group of young, therapeutically oriented people *"who connected with one another through these meditations, in order to take those meditations deeper into themselves and to understand them,"* and they proceed from the absolute reality of the spiritually created fact that accompanies that assumption—regardless of what was or was not really able to come into physical reality and instead remained within the sphere of pure intentions. Helene von Grunelius's early death in Arlesheim shook Wegman deeply, and for some time. On the other hand, Ita Wegman received from Grunelius's individuality an ongoing accompaniment in her work and experienced the unbroken interest of the deceased woman during the work in Arlesheim, feeling her often as a "guardian spirit" at her side in the Clinical Therapeutic Institute (letter from Ita Wegman to Jürgen von Grone, Dec. 16, 1937[39]).

~

If one takes up the knowledge, even a little bit, of the historical conditions briefly outlined, or rather hinted at, here, one gets a dim sense of the broader context for the efforts that are living in them—a context that gains in depth and drama when one further considers the sweeping historical events of the time, what happened in 1923 and 1924 in Dornach and in the world,[40] what Rudolf Steiner was campaigning for up to the end, and what even now has only been partially perceived, understood, and penetrated. It would seem sensible to think about these circumstances, which seem to belong firmly to the past, particularly in regard to their connection with the Warmth Meditation—regardless of the fact that the tangible content of the Warmth Meditation is fully independent of them. This preoccupation with and analysis of memories has a moral character that is all too easy to overlook, and it leads to a greater consciousness of the striving and the sacrifices that had once been and are still spiritually bound up in words that have been set down in print and have superficially reached the depersonalized space of being "available to all."

One might ask whether there is not a relative or even absolute obligation here to gain some "historical" knowledge inwardly, insofar as one—because of an individual situation or motivation—decides in the present to have some temporary or lasting contact with the text of the Warmth Meditation, a meditation dedicated as few others have been to a particular circle of people and that was entrusted to them in an unusually strict sense. This "historical" knowledge shall, as such, neither promise nor find an entry into the actual meditative process; but it nevertheless has, in a certain sense, both a preparatory and reflective character, it is an occurrence in one's surroundings, and as such, an occurrence that is part of the relationship to the spiritual world, to the beings and individuals who live within it.

In a certain sense, the same thing is true for the following considerations and suggestions that deal with certain spiritual-ideational aspects of the meditation. They also do not constitute the actual experiential space of the meditative exercise, which can be more fully realized on the far side of ideational foreknowledge and of any awareness of the contemporary situation;[41] indeed, the meditative exercise can, in a sense, *detach from situation and occurrence.* ("The true meditation, the true exercise of the soul, lies not in the theoretical, intellectual content of a meditation, but rather in its mantric character. The mantric character comes when the sense of the meditation detaches from situation and occurrence, when the human being separates from the intellectual content and departs from itself...."[42])

At the same time, it should not be overlooked how much Rudolf Steiner intended, in the course for young medical practitioners, to describe systematically to his audience the ideational implications of each of the course's mantras, which is possibly connected with the fact that each of the mantras in the lectures for young medical practitioners followed a very specific intention based in the particulars of their profession—which is to say that they were not personal meditations but were rather formulated and understood as exact, goal-oriented directives from Rudolf Steiner. ("*In the case of the meditations, the real point is that one truly wants, inwardly wants, to practice medicine, to the point that one says to oneself: this is the path, and now I will turn to this meditation as often as I can. I am conscious of the fact that when I complete one or the other of them, it is for a particular purpose.*"[43])

Steiner described this character of the exercises following a question from Helene von Grunelius on April 22, 1924; and the letter from her to Margarthe Bockholt from August 21, 1924, which was cited extensively above, demonstrates how Grunelius sought to work with the ideational connections and contents of the Warmth Meditation, sometimes in an almost desperate fashion. At the time this letter was written, Grunelius had been working with the text of the meditation for over seventeen months, wrestling with it and striving for ever-deeper levels of experience, just as Rudolf Steiner indicated when he said: "*You must attempt to live evermore deeply into the essence of this meditation, to connect yourself with it more strongly....*"

The Warmth Meditation

Preparation: How do I find the Good?

1. Can I think the Good?

   I cannot think the Good.
   Thinking is brought about by my ether body.
   My ether body works in the fluidity of my body.
   So I do not find the Good in the fluidity of the body.

2. Can I feel the Good?

   I can certainly feel the Good, but it is not there
   through me if I only feel it.
   Feeling is brought about by my astral body.
   My astral body works in the air element
   of my body.
   So I do not find the Good that exists through me
   in the air element of the body.

3. Can I will the Good?

   I can will the Good.
   Willing is brought about by my "I".
   My "I" works in the warmth ether of my body.
   So I can realize the Good physically in the warmth.

[Meditation]: I feel my humanity in my warmth.

1. I feel light in my warmth.

   (Take care that this sensation of light emerges in the region where the physical heart is.)

2. I feel the substance of the world resonating in my warmth.

   (Take care that the unusual sound-sensation, spreading out into the whole body, goes from the lower body to the head.)

3. I feel in my head the world-life moving in my warmth.

   (Take care that the unusual sensation of life spreads from the head to the whole body.)

II

Spiritual Connections

You detect at this point what life, which has poured into the world, actually is. Where can the source of this life be found? It can be found in what stirs the moral ideals and prompts us to say that, if we allow ourselves to be filled by the light of moral ideals today, they will bear life and matter and light, and create worlds. We carry that world-creating element, and the moral ideal is the source of all that creates worlds.

—Rudolf Steiner[44]

Herr Dr. said to me recently: you must try to live more fully into the essence of this meditation, to connect yourself more strongly with it, and then what you seek will come (he said something along those lines).

I was not at all clear about how I was to do that. In my first days here I mostly read that book by Wachsmuth, which is truly wonderful and illuminated my thoughts. Apart from that, I read our medical course from Easter, but that only made me more doubtful. In the first few days I felt worse from day to day, until I actually got to the point of feeling sick. My temperature rose somewhat, and then I stayed completely in bed for two days. Once I started to feel a little better, I lay on a sofa on the balcony or, when it was too cold outside, in the room. I then read the three lectures from December 1920, which are actually quite connected with the meditation. At first, I felt like nothing made sense, until suddenly, in the morning of the day before yesterday, when I was reading the lecture cycle on the Gospel of Luke again, the lights came on for me. Since then, I have also felt almost completely healthy!

—Helene von Grunelius to Margarethe Bockholt

Helene von Grunelius wrestled for a long time intensively with the spiritual content of the Warmth Meditation, whose beauty and superficial simplicity she had experienced very early. She studied Anthroposophy; in August 1924 she studied the book from Guenther Wachmuth that had been published at the beginning of that same year (with a title page illustration from Rudolf Steiner) on the formative etheric forces of the cosmos, earth, and human being; she repeatedly studied the so-called "Bridge Lectures" around Christmastime in Dornach, from December 17th to the 19th, 1920, which she had heard (along with others, including Madeleine van Deventer, Ita Wegman, and Willem Zylmans van Emmichoven)—the transcript of which Helene von Grunelius had requested from Rudolf Steiner in preparation for the course for the group of young medical practitioners.

Shortly before the last September meeting in 1924, which she considered so very important, Helene von Grunelius studied the great Christological course on the

Gospel of Luke, which Rudolf Steiner had given back in September 1909 in Basel. She studied it as part of her search for a Luke-inspired aspect of future medical work, which Rudolf Steiner had hinted at during the Easter course by emphasizing that the Gospel of Luke was written with a decidedly medical slant. ("*We must be absolutely clear about this; since the Gospel of Luke has not yet really been taken up as an inner directive for the will to heal—this matter has not yet been understood—the result is that actually, within our current mode of thinking, there lives no Christian will to heal, but rather a will to heal that has been scuttled in our spiritual culture of Arabism, which has embraced Christianity with a pair of forceps.*"[45])

Helene von Grunelius also studied the lectures from the Gospel of Luke course in Basel in her efforts to grasp the deeper spiritual content of the Warmth Meditation. To be sure, experiences had long ago been bestowed upon her in connection with these meditative exercises that strengthened her conviction on her path and connected her more deeply with the Mystery of human incarnation as well as with the willed path to realizing the *Good*. But Rudolf Steiner had also told her the actual, final goal of the meditation and indicated that it was the concrete "*path for medical practitioners to behold the etheric Christ.*" In other words, the goal was an incredibly significant (perhaps the most significant) experience of individual perception in the twentieth century, formulated in specific terms related to a particular profession—a designated goal that raised many questions and was hardly easy to achieve.

Esoteric Christology was a hidden theme in the life of Helene von Grunelius (and those of her generation[46]), a theme that emerged only very seldom; but when it did, it was explicitly articulated and communicated, as for example in November 1923, when she tried to assist her younger friend Madeleine van Deventer in the dire straits of her materialistically inflected medical study, and in so doing revealed some of her own path. In Grunelius's letter from this period, she writes:

> So, Maddy, keep your chin up; if you can manage to maintain your inner enthusiasm through this period of time when you have to work in the clinics, then you will have gained a strong, driving inner force, and you will be even more connected with Anthroposophy. Try, as I did this summer in Frankfurt when I was so unhappy, because I noticed from day to day how inwardly beaten down I was and how much strength I was losing as everything around me and in me grew darker. Then, [I] always thought: I must be conscious of

> and suffer this pain, this feeling Christ felt when crucified, in order to receive an impulse to fight for salvation. And then I experienced truly what it means to receive an impulse for spiritual science through the study of natural science. From that period on, I knew what enthusiasm [*Begeisterung*] is—I knew what a true and genuine power it is.[47]

Helene von Grunelius wanted to suffer, as he did, the pains of Christ's crucifixion consciously and deeply, "in order to receive an impulse to fight for salvation"[48]—a formulation from 1923 that she used to describe her inner path through a difficult struggle with materialistic natural science and its impact on medicine. Almost involuntarily, in this unusual remark from a medical student who had only just turned twenty-six in the first quarter of the twentieth century, something was expressed that is intimately connected with one of the central tasks for the future of human civilization and for the sphere of the healing arts.

As Rudolf Steiner had described in some detail ten years earlier in London, at the culmination of the natural scientific-materialist civilization of the nineteenth century[49]—which had made great demands on and called for great responsibility from medicine—there occurred a "*second crucifixion*" of Christ in the spiritual world, an annihilation of the cosmic Christ-consciousness through destructive earthly influences. ("*Evermore, when people went through the gates of death and entered the spiritual world, they took with them the results of their materialistic ideas on earth, such that after the sixteenth century, more and more seeds of earthly materials were carried over.*"[50]) This subsequently resulted in the immanent preconditions for a second resurrection of the Christ-being in the sphere of earthly human consciousness. Following an impressive description of all that is connected with these processes,[51] Rudolf Steiner remarks on the particulars as follows:

> The seeds of earthly materialism, which have been carried into the spiritual world more and more since the sixteenth century by souls moving through the gates of death and have brought about ever more darkness, form the black sphere of materialism. Christ has taken this black sphere into his being, in the spirit of Manichean principles, in order to transform it. It has brought about the "spiritual asphyxiation" of the angelic beings through whom the Christ-being was revealed since the Mystery of Golgotha. This sacrifice of Christ in the nineteenth century is comparable to his sacrifice on the physical plane at the Mystery of Golgotha and can

> be referred to as the second crucifixion of Christ on the etheric plane. This spiritual asphyxiation, which precipitated the dissolution of the consciousness of those angelic beings, is a repetition of the Mystery of Golgotha in the world that lies directly behind our own so that a resurrection of the Christ-consciousness, which had been hidden, might take place in human souls. This resurrection will become the clairvoyant vision of humanity in the twentieth century.[52]

In the same lecture cycle, as well as numerous later remarks, Rudolf Steiner describes the extent to which this future beholding of the Christ in the etheric can be considered a "*new revelation of Michael*"[53] and is, in fact, inwardly and directly connected with the Michaelic battle for the future of civilization on earth (and the inspiration for a new, spiritualized scientific culture). Michael prepares the way for the coming Christ, insofar as he "*leads a battle in the spiritual world*," a "*battle for the purity of the spiritual horizon*," that is in service of the "*pure emergence of the future, etheric Christ*"[54] and that implies the conquest over enduring harmful influences that might affect the human constitution, particularly ones coming from the ahrimanic sphere into human science and civilization. According to Rudolf Steiner, the influence of these adversaries can have even more harmful effects in the spiritual world after death and it will take the efforts of human beings in the service of Michael to defeat them. Helene von Grunelius's inner impulse "to fight for salvation" for both medicine and human civilization and her impulse to serve with all of her power the realization of the Good "*on the path of the will*,"[55] point to the clear signature of her young generation, whose particular spirituality "*at the beginning of the Michaelic age*" Rudolf Steiner had remarked upon on multiple occasions.[56]

~

Early on, Rudolf Steiner drew medical practitioners' attention to the paramount significance of warmth and the system of warmth in the human being, not only for understanding generally the body's structure (including its evolutionary aspects), but also for penetrating more deeply into the relationship between the soul-spiritual and the living physical aspects, right down to the will dimensions of our intentional actions and our morally infused existence. As early as March 1911, in *An Occult Physiology*, a medical lecture cycle that Rudolf Steiner delivered to an audience made up primarily of doctors in Prague, he said:

> In the warming processes of the blood, we can see the direct expression of the highest level—that of the "I"—and under that play out the other processes of the human organism. The warming process is...the highest; in it, the "I"–soul activity is active. As a result, a transformation of our "I"–soul activity results in a feeling of growing inwardly warm, which can then turn into a feeling of growing physically warm in the blood. And so we see how the soul-spiritual, moving down from above through the warming process, takes holds in the organic, in the physiological, and we could further point to many other instances of how the soul-spiritual makes contact with the organic through the warming process.[57]

More than eleven years later, in October 1922, in the course of his first conversation with the medical student group around Helene von Grunelius (she herself was absent because of her exams), Steiner discussed this spiritual-physiological connection. Having heard from the students that, in light of the materialistic tendencies of civilization, they wanted to begin humanitarian work for all of human civilization, Rudolf Steiner emphasized the specific medical task of the people standing before him, warned them against abstract psychological morality and further prompted them to take the foundational aspect of warmth as the starting point for their medical, therapeutic thinking and activity. According to notes made by medical student Manfred von Fries about the conversation, Steiner said:

> You must find the bridges from the medical-scientific to the moral, to love. You see, when I speak, for example, about what I am calling the warmth organization of the human being, this is, at first, merely an abstraction for you. But you must then find the bridge that will allow you to experience this warmth organization such that you find your way from the differentiations in the warmth of various organs to *moral warmth*. You must learn to experience what we call a "warm heart" in such a way as to actually feel this warm heart within the physical realm. You must find your way out of the scientific-physiological into the spiritual-moral realm, and also from the spiritual-moral back into the physiological-anatomical realm.[58]

The first lecture course of Rudolf Steiner's, which Helene von Grunelius heard with great interest, took place in the first two weeks of March 1920 in the rooms of the Stuttgart Waldorf School. It again centered on a particular theme that also extended into the physical: "Warmth on the border between positive and negative materiality." Nine months after that, she had worked her way through the Bridge Lectures (mentioned previously) in the Dornach *Schreinerei,* which, in their general tone and style, are effectively a prelude to the talks given three years later to the young medical practitioners at the Christmas Conference. The human being as a cosmic-social being and the relationship of the moral sphere to the physical organization of the world were the main themes of the lectures that Rudolf Steiner held in Dornach beginning at the end of November 1920.

Seven days before Christmas Eve, Steiner then began to focus his prior remarks on the physiological organization of the human being in a new dynamic that was initially surprising for the audience members. On December 17, 1920, he spoke for the first time about the divisions of the human being and the basic organizational levels of the physical body—the warmth, air, liquid, and solid systems—in which the spiritual divisions are physically and etherically realized and thereby make possible the soul development of the human being. Regarding will activity and its connection with the "I"-infused warmth organization, he said:

> The "I" itself is, I would suggest, that spiritual structure which, on its own, directs and configures the warmth that we bear within ourselves—and it does not simply configure it by shaping its external

> boundaries, but rather configures it from within. And the soul element—we cannot understand that if we do not consider the direct effects of the "I" on warmth. The "I" is first and foremost that within human beings which sets the will in motion and lends to it its impulses. How does the "I" generate will impulses? We have already discussed, from another point of view, how the will impulses are connected with the terrestrial, as opposed to the thought impulses, the impulses of the imagination, which are connected with the extraterrestrial. But though the "I" is connected intimately with the will impulses, how does it infuse these will impulses into the organism, into the whole of the human being? This can happen because the will is active within the warmth system of the human being. When the "I" has a will impulse, this will impulse works first upon the warmth system.... The thing that busies itself within this warmth, that makes the warmth flow and gives it an inner movement, the thing that actually makes it an organized system—that is the "I."[59]

Every will activity in the human organization comes about because of the "I" working through the system of warmth.[60] However, according to Rudolf Steiner on December 12, 1920, in Dornach, moral ideals create over and above that an inner *excitation* and *enlivening* of the warmth system ("*You must imagine this as a concrete process: enthusiasm for a moral ideal, enlivening of the warmth system.*"[61]), enlivening that connects with the rest of the levels of the incarnated human organization and leads to light-etheric alterations in the aeriform system, to etheric-sound changes ("*sound sources*") in the liquid organism and to life-etheric changes ("*seeds of life*") in the solid organism.

> When a moral ideal enlivens the warmth, because warmth is active throughout the whole organism and in all organisms, it affects the aeriform system as well. But this effect on the aeriform system is not only warming; rather, when the warmth, which becomes active in the warmth system, affects the human aeriform organism, it bestows upon it something to which I can refer only as a source of light. Seeds of light, so to speak, connect with the aeriform organism, such that the moral ideal which excites the warmth organism, elicits light sources in the aeriform organism.[62]

This enlivening also has great significance for the Being of the human after death and for the evolution of the earth and the cosmos:

> We see... how, in fact, our entire organism, beginning with the warmth system, is infused with

moral impulses. And when, in death, we depart from our physical body, our etheric body, our astral body, our "I," then in these higher level of human nature, we are infused with the influences that we had previously had. We were in our warmth system with our "I," inasmuch as moral ideals enlivened our warmth organism. We were in our aeriform organism, where light sources were planted that now go with us into the cosmos following our death. We excited in our liquid organism the tones that become the music of the spheres, which we ring out into the cosmos. We bring life out with us when we move through the gates of death.

You detect at this point what life, which has poured into the world, actually is. Where can the source of this life to be found? It can be found in what stirs the moral ideals and prompts us to say that, if we allow ourselves to be filled by the light of moral ideals today, they will bear life and matter and light, and create worlds. We carry that world-creating element, and the source of all that creates worlds is the moral ideal.[63]

Rudolf Steiner said to Helene von Grunelius prior to the course for the young medical practitioners that she should try to *light a fire* in the others with her *enthusiasm*[64]—in the Bridge Lectures from Christmas, 1920, he showed (in the manner referred to above) how such a moral enthusiasm can affect the human physiology and the world's process of becoming—how it can affect the furthering of the cosmogenetic process of evolution (when he spoke about warmth, light, sound, and life)—but he also showed how it is able to affect that spiritual sphere in which the Christ-being (with Michael's aid) can be revealed again (through a second *resurrection*).

~

In this way, Rudolf Steiner introduced the young medical practitioners through the course proceedings and mantric exercises from January and April 1924 to the essential being of the elements, to their *physical and etheric conditions*, guiding them through an important step in gaining knowledge and experience of the "*old holy Mysteries.*"[65] But the most encompassing aspect—the one that initiates things and bears the greatest load—is warmth—that qualitative warmth that Rudolf Steiner also spoke about so often during the esoteric lessons following the Christmas Conference, that all-encompassing warmth that is "*inwardly fully connected*" with human beings and their inmost nature, that warmth in which they live and move as in no other element.[66] The path to warmth brings about not only the first evolutionary steps of the future earth organism, but also the spiritual pre-formation of the future heart as the central organ of human formation[67] as well as the gradual "I"-incarnation of the human being on earth.

Rudolf Steiner spoke during an esoteric class in 1924 on the *warming force that awakens the self*[68] and on the fire that *lights the flame* of the human "I".[69] Again and again, he emphasizes the intimate relationship between this "I"-element and human morality, and with that the relationship between this "I"-element and the future significance of an individual's destiny in his or her current life.

According to Rudolf Steiner, in the warming processes, not only the retrospective biographical examination of the individual after death but also the life-historical interiorization of what was experienced and carried, as well as what was purely intended as part of an individual existence—all of this is fully realized in the warming processes. The physically realized actions in both their good ("*the good that exists through me*") and their destructive aspects, as well as the intentions to act are changed, according to Rudolf Steiner, into the *delicate warmth structures* of the heart[70] and as such belong to the on-going, uninterrupted process of human becoming, to the transformation of the temporal into the eternal and of the eternal into the temporal.[71] The forces awakened by these processes (also in the etheric structures of light, sound, and life) encounter, during the postmortem Being of the human, the cosmic world order and the higher beings who are part of the hierarchy of that realm, whose directive forces lie at the foundation of both the world and human incarnation—through enduring, ongoing acts of sacrifice and through the *fire of creative love*,[72] which makes possible the divine continuance of the Good.

Rudolf Steiner led the young medical practitioners onto the spiritual–psychological path of warmth into the sphere of the etheric body and its differentiated qualities—a body that not only unites the therapeutic life forces of the human being and stands at the center of all therapeutic efforts,[73] but that also, in its inner substance, is an essential organism formed out of the forces of love: a true "*body of love*."[74] According to further remarks from Rudolf Steiner, the Christ-impulse of the Mystery of Golgotha streams into this receptive human etheric body of formative forces, and brings about its successive reinvigoration and infusion, which are themselves the preconditions for the continuing evolution of the Earth as well as for a different, future state of human health.[75] At the same time, according to Rudolf Steiner, the vitalizing changes to human bodily life that this brings about allow for the perception of the etheric Christ, two thousands years after the events at Golgotha. ("*When the etheric body is re-enlivened, it beholds the Christ.*"[76]) In other words, these changes become the organ that bears the Christ-experience "*in the etheric body.*"[77]

The individual who is morally sensitive, who acts responsibly, and who engages in spiritual practice, can—in the sense of the Warmth Meditation—activate the four types of the etheric in his or her etheric body and develop them into an organ of perception for the Christ-being. "The etheric body becomes independent in this way and can become an 'organ' that understands how to look about in its etheric surroundings" (Madeleine van Deventer[78]).

The image of the Christ-being that is accessible to human beings in the etheric is, according to Rudolf Steiner, woven from the purest and highest etheric forces, the elements of the sound and life etheric, which (according to the Basel lectures on the Gospel of Luke) were the sole etheric qualities to withdraw from the sphere of the adversarial luciferic forces during the early stages of earthly evolution and, as such, formed (and continue to form) the unbroken and protected "*tree of life*" that has been entrusted to the future.[79]

In this sense, the exercise given by Rudolf Steiner to Helene von Grunelius implied a meditative initiation into the sphere of activity of the etheric qualities and life processes that are united in the super-organzation of a warmth body and that are highly relevant to anyone with a medical orientation—an initiation that leads toward the "*world life that circles about us as the music of the spheres*" that Rudolf Steiner spoke of during an esoteric class[80] and stands in intimate connection to the paths of both the present and future Christ-experience and its continuing activity.

The Warmth Meditation was intended to allow Helene von Grunelius and her friends to find "*the path of the medical practitioner to behold the etheric Christ*" through the enlightened life forces of an educated and perceptive mode of thinking; as such, it was and is a central aid for the development of Christian medicine, which is infused with a truly therapeutic morality and a willingness to make ready sacrifices for the realization of the Good (which in turn directly promotes the individual *world-life*)[81] and deals appropriately with the various therapeutic qualities and forces in the world. It was intended, in this sense, quite clearly to promote and to support those therapeutic efforts that were undertaken through individual efforts with a responsibility for the workings of the Christ-being and that have an effect on the present and future Being of the human—of the diseased human living in a threatened world.

Appendix

Original transcript of the Warmth Meditation
by Rudolf Steiner

Copy of the Warmth Meditation
by Ita Wegman

Vorbereitung: Wie finde ich das Gute?

1. Kann ich das Gute denken?

Ich kann das Gute nicht denken.

Denken versorgt mein Aetherleib.

Mein Aetherleib wirkt in der Flüssigkeit meines Leibes.

Also in der Flüssigkeit des Leibes finde ich das Gute nicht.

2. Kann ich das Gute fühlen?

Ich kann das Gute zwar fühlen; aber es ist durch mich nicht da, wenn ich es nur fühle.

Fühlen versorgt mein astralischer Leib.

Mein astralischer Leib wirkt in dem Luftförmigen meines Leibes.

Also in dem Luftförmigen des Leibes finde ich das durch mich existierende Gute nicht.

3. Kann ich das Gute wollen?

Ich kann das Gute wollen.

Wollen versorgt mein Ich

Mein Ich wirkt in dem Wärmeaether meines Leibes.

Also in der Wärme kann ich das Gute physisch verwirklichen.

Rudolf Steiner's handwriting, page 1

Ich fühle meine Menschheit in meiner Wärme.

1. Ich fühle Licht in meiner Wärme.

[Acht geben, dass diese Lichtempfindung auftritt in der Gegend, wo das physische Herz ist]

2. Ich fühle tönend die Weltschöpfung in meiner Wärme.

[Acht geben, dass die eigentümliche Ton-Empfindung vom Unterleib nach dem Kopfe, aber mit Ausbreitung im ganzen Leibe geht.]

3. Ich fühle in meinem Kopfe sich regend das Weltenleben in meiner Wärme.

[Acht geben, dass die eigentümliche Lebensempfindung vom Kopfe nach dem ganzen Körper sich verbreitet]

Rudolf Steiner's handwriting, page 2

Vorbereitung

1/ Wie finde ich das Gute?
Kan̄ ich das Gute denken?
Ich kan̄ das Gute nicht denken
Denken versorgt mein Aetherleib
Mein Aetherleib wirkt in der Flüssigkeit
meines Leibes
Also in der Flüssigkeit meines Leibes finde ich
Gute nicht.

2/ Kan̄ ich das Gute fühlen?
Ich kan̄ das Gute zwar fühlen aber es ist durch
mich nicht da, wen̄ ich es nur fühle.
Fühlen versorgt mein astralischer Leib
Mein astralischer Leib wirkt in dem Luftförmige
meines Leibes
Also in dem Luftförmigen des Leibes finde
~~Als~~ ich das durch mich existierende Gute nic

3/ Kan̄ ich das Gute wollen?
Ich kan̄ das Gute wollen
Wollen versorgt mein Ich
Mein Ich wirkt in dem Wärme Aether
meines Leibes
Also in der Wärme kan̄ ich das Gute
physisch verwirklichen.

—

Ita Wegman's handwriting, page 1

1) Ich fühle meine Menschheit in meiner Wärme
Ich fühle Licht in meiner Wärme
(Acht geben, dass diese Lichtempfindung
Auftritt in der Gegend, wo das physische
Herz ist)

2) Ich fühle tönend die Weltsubstanz in
meiner Wärme
(Acht geben, dass die eigentümliche Ton-Empfindung
vom Unterleib nach dem Kopfe, aber
mit Ausbreitung im ganzen Körper geht)

3) Ich fühle in meinem Kopf sich regend
das Weltenleben in meiner Wärme
(Acht geben das die eigentümliche
Lebensempfindung vom Kopfe
nach dem ganzen Körper sich
verbreitet)

Nabel

Ita Wegman's handwriting, page 2

Notes

1. See also Konrad Gaiser. *Platons ungeschriebene Lehre.* Stuttgart 1968, pp. 6 and 452 (Testimonia Platonica, Appendix 7). Aristotle's writings on "the Good" is one of the transcripts (Hypomnemata) of the platonic lectures that was supposed to remain in the school's possession but was eventually circulated more widely.
2. See also Sergej O. Prokofieff. *Die Grundsteinmeditation. Ein Schlüssel zu den neuen cristlichen Mysterien.* Dornach 2003, p. 38. [E: *The Foundation Stone Meditation: A Key to the Christian Mysteries* (London: Temple Lodge, 2006)].
3. Cited in Rudolf Steiner. *Die Konstitution der Allgemeinen Anthroposophischen Gesellschaft und der Freien Hochschule fur Geisteswissenschaft.* CW 260a. Dornach 1987, p. 36.
4. Rudolf Steiner, *Mantrische Sprüche. Seelenübungen II.* CW 268. Dornach 1999, pp. 296f. [E: *Mantric Sayings: Meditations 1903–1925* (Great Barrington, MA: SteinerBooks, 2015)].
5. Madeleine van Deventer, *Die anthroposophisch-medizinische Bewegung in den verschiedenen Etappen ihrer Entwicklung.* Arlesheim 1992, p. 24.
6. Both sheets can be found in the Rudolf Steiner Archive in Dornach and bear the numbers 3221 and 4470. A transcription of Rudolf Steiner's handwritten pages and a facsimile reproduction of both sheets were first published by the administration of Rudolf Steiner's estate [*Nachlassverwaltung*] in 1999 in the volume *Mantrische Sprüche.*

Seelenübungen II (CW 268, see note 4). For the rights to reproduce the original facsimile of the handwritten pages in the appendix of this book, my thanks go to Dr. Walter Kugler.

7 See Peter Selg (ed.), *Anthroposophische Arzte. Lebens und Arbeitswege im 20. Jahrhundert.* Dornach 2000, pp. 249ff. (Afterword by Marianne Fiechtr-Bischoff and Gudrune Wolff-Hoffmann), and Bodo von Plato (ed.), *Anthroposophie im 20. Jahrhundert.* Dornach 2003, pp. 146f. (Afterword by Joop van Darn). A comprehensive appraisal of Madeleine van Deventer's life work as well as a new edition of her essays and studies is in preparation through the Ita Wegman Institute.

8 See note 5. Madeleine van Deventer's later review of anthroposophical medicine's historical development was determined in part by her concerns about the spiritual quality of future work. Even in October 1981, van Deventer herself introduced the retreat day for doctors at the Goetheanum, "The Spiritualization of Curative Arts in the Present," and one year later she ended her text with the reflective sentences: "The anthroposophical medical movement has expanded in an astonishing way in recent decades. Evidently, many souls have now incarnated who already, from their lives before birth, carry a great longing for a new form of healing. Will these souls now find in our movement that very thing they have sought? How can we carry forward in a dynamic way this new form of healing that Rudolf Steiner brought us and that was put into practice so intensively on earth by Ita Wegman?" (van Deventer, p. 67).

9 See Peter Selg, *Helene von Grunelius und Rudolf Steiners Kurse für junge Mediziner. Eine biographische Studie.* Dornach 2003; *Die Briefkorrespondenz der "Jungen Mediziner." Eine dokumentarische Studie zur Rezeption von Rudolf Steiners "Jungmediziner"-Kursen.* Dornach 2005;

"Die Medizin muss Ernst machen mit dem geistigen Leben." Rudolf Steiners Hochschulkurse fur die "Jungen Mediziner." Dornach 2006.

10 "I recall a gathering of Rudolf Steiner, Ita Wegman, and the clinic's assistant doctors in the carpenter's workshop. Apart from my brother and me, one or two other students were present. The topic was Rudolf Steiner's suggestion that we should take a notebook and write down what a professor said, or a good medical case, on the left-hand side, so that we could transpose the symptoms of the illness into the language of various aspects of the human being. Rudolf Steiner gave the following example of this: '*The patient has edema in the right half of his body*' would be transposed to, '*Weakness of the etheric in the lower half of the body.*'" (Madeleine van Deventer, p. 22).

11 Ibid., p. 24.

12 The questions that van Deventer poses about Grunelius only ostensibly contradict Manfred von Kreis's record of a conversation recorded immediately following a meeting with Rudolf Steiner in Stuttgart on 10/29/1922 (reprinted as a facsimilie in my monograph on Helene von Grunelius [see note 9] on p. 30), in which the so-called "double accounting" (one traditional medical diagnosis and one spiritual scientific diagnosis) of the older anthroposophical doctors was rigorously discarded. In fact, the photocopied record comes from Helene von Grunelius's estate, who apparently, immediately after receiving it, maintained in a handwitten note in the margin that the process criticized by this circle referred to a recommendation that came explicitly from Rudolf Steiner ("Recommendation from Steiner/transposing")—and further attempted to actually implement the procedure Steiner offered, even if she did not do so to her own satisfaction. Madeleine van Deventer used this record (and the marginalia from Helene von Grunelius, as well as

the concept of "transposing" Steiner proposed) in the draft of her memoirs, citing from it liberally (without giving the source).

13 In the further development of van Deventer's worthy text, there are certain other imprecise details that do not stand up to documentary review. For example, when reading the chapter on the "young medical professionals movement," one should consider that the "disinvitation"of Maria Hachez and Erna van Deventer-Wolfram from the Easter course (see pp. 27f.) that van Deventer so decidedly and vividly describes, actually refers to the Pastoral-Medicine course. It can be verified that Maria Hachez attended the lectures in April 1924, though Erna von Deventer-Wolfran (as well as her husband Henk) had a scheduling conflict at Easter (Ita Wegman Archive).

14 Peter Selg, *Helene von Grunelius*, p. 36 (author's emphasis).

15 Ita Wegman Archive, Arlesheim.

16 Published in Rudolf Steiner. *Die Erkenntnis-Aufgabe der Jugend.* CW 217a. Dornach 1981, pp. 205ff. [E: *Youth and the Etheric Heart: Rudolf Steiner Speaks to the Younger Generation* (Great Barrington, MA: SteinerBooks, 2007)].

17 See Rudolf Steiner. *Die Geschichte und die Bedingungen der anthroposophischen Bewegung im Verhältnis zur Anthroposophischen Gesellschaft.* CW 258. Dornach 1981.

18 Peter Selg. *Helene von Grunelius*, pp. 38ff.

19 Ibid.

20 Ita Wegman Archive, Arlesheim.

21 Peter Selg, p. 50.

22 See Emanuel Zeylmans van Emmichoven. *Wer war Ita Wegman. Eine Dokumentation. Band I.* Dornach 2000, pp. 144ff [E: *Who Was Ita Wegman: A Documentation,* vol. 1 (Chestnut Ridge, NY: Mercury, 1995)]; *"Die Erkraftung des Herzens." Rudolf Steiners Zusammenarbeit mit Ita Wegman.* Arlesheim 2009.

23 Rudolf Steiner. *Meditative Betrachtungen und Anleitungen zu einer Vertiefung der Heilkunst.* CW 316. Dornach 2003, p. 135. [E: *Understanding Healing: Meditative Reflections on Deepening Medicine through Spiritual Science* (Great Barrington, MA: SteinerBooks, 2014)].

24 Peter Selg. *"Ich bin fur Fortschreiten," Ita Wegman und die Medizinische Sektion.* Dornach 2004. [E: *I Am for Going Ahead: Ita Wegman's Work for the Social Ideals of Anthroposophy* (Great Barrington, MA: SteinerBooks, 2012)].

25 See Peter Selg. *"Die Medizin muss Ernst machen mit dem geistigen Leben." Rudolf Steiners Hochschulkurse für die "Jungen Mediziner."* Dornach 2006.

26 Rudolf Steiner. *Meditative Betrachtungen und Anleitungen zu einer Vertiefung der Heilkunst*, p. 224.

27 Ita Wegman Archive, Arlesheim.

28 Peter Selg. *Helene von Grunelius*, p. 109.

29 See Peter Selg. *Die Briefkorrespondenz der "Jungen Mediziner." Eine dokumentarische Studie zur Rezeption von Rudolf Steiners "Jungmediziner"-Kursen.* Dornach 2005.

30 Peter Selg. *Helene von Grunelius*, p. 110.

31 On August 25, Margarthe Bockholt shared with Helen von Grunelius, for example, that Ita Wegman had told her she was to give the Warmth Meditation to Julia Bort, and went on to write, "I will certainly do it, but perhaps you can tell her some things in September as well. It is wonderful that she is to receive it; then she will really be part of things" (Ita Wegman Archive, Arlesheim).

32 Peter Selg. *Helene von Grunelius*, p. 112.

33 See Rudolf Steiner. *Das Zusammenwirken von Arzten und Seelsorgern. Pastoral-Medizinischer Kurs.* CW 318. Dornach 1994, pp. 165ff. [E: *Broken Vessels: The Spiritual Structure of Human Frailty* (Great Barrington, MA: SteinerBooks, 2002)].

34 See, however, Peter Selg, *Die Briefkorrespondenz der Jungen Mediziner. Einedokumentarische Studie zur Rezeption-von Rudolf Steiners "Jungmediziner"-Kursen*, Dornach 2005; *"Die Medizin muss Ernst machen mit dem geistigen Leben." Rudolf Steiners Hochschulkurse für die "jungen Mediziner."* Dornach 2006, pp. 145ff.

35 Ibid., pp. 153ff.

36 See Carl Bessenich, Paul Bühler, Otto Eckstein, Curt Englert-Faye, Otto Fränkl, Emil Grosheintz, Ehrenfried Pfeiffer, Hermann Poppelbaum, Paul Eugen Schiller, Günther Schubert, Richard Schubert and Jan Stuten. *Denkschrift über Angelegenheiten der Anthroposophischen Gesellschaft in den Jahren 1925 bis 1935.* Dornach 1935. Reprinted in Zeylmans, Band 3, pp. 259ff.

37 Rudolf Steiner. *Das Zusammenwirken von Arzten und Seelsorgern. Pastoral-Medizinischer Kurs*, p. 124. [E: *Broken Vessels: The Spiritual Structure of Human Frailty* (Great Barrington, MA: SteinerBooks, 2002)].

38 Ita Wegman Archive, Arlesheim.

39 Ibid.

40 See, among others, my study *"Das Jahr 1923,"* in Peter Selg. *Gerhard Kienle. Leben und Werk. Band I. Eine Biographie.* Dornach 2003, pp. 25ff.; as well as (regarding the events and proceedings in Dornach) the two volumes of documents edited by Hella Wiesberger: *Das Schicksalsjahr 1923 in der Geschichte der Anthroposophischen Gesellschaft* (CW 259) and *Die Konstitution der Allgemeinen Anthroposophischen Gesellschaft und der Freien Hochschule fur Geisteswissenschaft. Der Wiederaufbau des Goetheanum* (CW 260a).

41 In reference to a question from Ilse Knauer ("What must I do out of my "I" when I do a meditation?"), Rudolf Steiner remarked in the Easter course for young medical practitioners: "Now, you see, meditation consists of the following: as modern human beings, you have this feeling in regard to

every sentence, you have to understand it. This is an explicit activity of the 'I' in our present incarnations. Everything that you do intellectually is an explicit activity of the 'I.' The intellect [predominates] in our present incarnations, and everything else is covered up by the 'I,' working at most in a dreamlike and unconscious way. On the other hand, meditation means turning off this intellectual striving and taking up the meditative content as it is given—purely, shall we say—according to what it literally contains. When you approach the meditative content intellectually, before taking it into yourself, you set your 'I' in motion, and then you actually start thinking about the content of the meditation—you have it outside of yourself. When you simply allow the content of the meditation as it is given to be present in your consciousness—not thinking about it, but simply allowing it to be present in your consciousness—then your 'I' works within you not out of its current incarnation, but out of its prior one. You hold your intellect still; you set yourself into the content of the words, which you hear inwardly, not outwardly, as the content of the words—you place yourself in that, and by doing so, your inner being works within the content of the meditation, the being that is not the being of your current incarnation. But this means that the content of the meditation is not something that you are to understand, but rather something that really works within you, and works within you such that you finally become aware that 'now I have experienced something that I could not experience before.' Take a simple meditation that I have often given you: 'Wisdom lives in light.' Now, you see, when you think about that, you can come up with all sorts of clever things, but also all sorts of terribly foolish things. It is there so that it can be heard inwardly: 'Wisdom lives in life.' When you hear that inwardly, something is paying attention that is not there because of your current incarnation, but because you brought it along with you from an earlier life on earth. And this part of you thinks and perceives, and it illuminates something within you after a while that you did not know before, something that you could not have come up with out of your intellect. Inwardly, you are much further along than your intellect. It encloses only a small portion of all that is there" (Rudolf Steiner, *Meditative Betrachtungen und Anleitungen zu einer Vertiefung der Heilkunst*, pp. 145f).

42 Rudolf Steiner. *Esoterische Unterweisungen für die erste Klasse der Freien Hochschule für Geisteswissenschaft am Goetheanum 1924*. CW 270. Band II. Dornach 1999, p. 41.

43 Rudolf Steiner. *Meditative Betrachtungen und Anleitungen zu einer Vertiefung der Heilkunst*, p. 159.

44 Rudolf Steiner. *Die Brücke zwischen der Weltgeistigkeit und dem Physischen des Menschen*. CW 202, Dornach 1993, p. 189. [E: *Universal Spirituality and Human Physicality: Bridging the Divide* (London: Rudolf Steiner Press, 2014)].

45 Rudolf Steiner. *Meditative Betrachtungen und Anleitungen zu einer Vertiefung der Heilkunst*, p. 192.

46 In his "Pädagogischen Jugendkurs" in October 1922 (and thus at the same time as the first meeting of anthroposophical medical students that would eventually lead to the January 1924 course in Dornach), Rudolf Steiner said regarding the Christologically oriented search for knowledge undertaken by the young generation sitting before him: "*If one were to set in clear words the things that play out chaotically in the depths of the soul, it would go something like this: in the depths of the soul, there is a striving to understand the Mystery of Golgotha again. A new Christ-experience is sought. We necessarily are standing before the new experience of the Christ-event. In its first form, it was still being experienced with the remainder of the old soul inheritances,*

but since these have been depleted since the fifteenth century, it has only been carried forward by tradition. In the last third of the nineteenth century, the darkening process was completed. No old inheritance remained. From out of this darkness of the human soul, a new light must be sought. The spiritual world must be experienced anew.—This is the significant experience that the deeper nature of the current youth movement imbues into the soul. It is therefore not only clear in a superficial way, but in a very deep sense, that something must now be experienced in the world historical development of humanity—something that comes utterly and completely out of human beings themselves" (Rudolf Steiner. *Geistige Wirkenskräfte im Zusammenleben von alter und junger Generation. Pädagogischer Jugendkurs.* CW 217. Dornach 1988, pp. 38f).

47 Peter Selg. *Helene von Grunelius*, p. 15.

48 On the spiritual aspects of this ahrimanically determined culmatination (around 1843/44), see especially Rudolf Steiner's remarks in the Apocalypse course for the priests of the Christian Community (*Apokalypsen und Priesterwirken.* CW 346. Dornach 1995, pp. 183f. [E: *The Book of Revelation: And the Work of the Priest* (London: Rudolf Steiner Press, 1999)]), as well as my symptomalogical-biographical study on *Johannes Müller im 19. Jahrhundert—Schicksal von Leben und Werk.* In Peter Selg. *Michael und Christus. Studien zur Anthroposophie Rudolf Steiners.* Arlesheim 2010, pp. 265–303.

49 See Peter Selg. "Die geistige Dimension des Menschen? Zur Entwicklung der medizinischen Anthropologie im 20. Jahrhundert." In Peter Heusser/Peter Selg. *Das Leib-Seele-Problem.* Arlesheim 2011.

50 Rudolf Steiner, *Vorstufen zum Mysterium von Golgatha.* CW 152. Dornach 1990, p. 45. [E: *Approaching the Mystery of Golgotha* (Great Barrington, MA: SteinerBooks, 2006)].

51 For more on things pertaining to these remarks from Rudolf Steiner, see the great overview work by Sergej O. Prokofieff, *Die Mysterien des ästherischen Christus in der Gegenwart.* In *Der Jahreskreislauf als Einweihungsweg zum Erleben der Christus-Wesenheit.* Stuttgart 1986, pp. 319ff (ch. 12); *Die Erscheinung des Christus im Ätherischen und das Wesen des Grundsteins der Weihnachtstagung 1923/1924.* In Thomas Stöckli (ed.). *Wege zur Christus-Erfahrung.* Dornach 1991, pp. 324ff.; *Das Erscheinen des Christus im Ätherischen*, Dornach 2010.

52 Rudolf Steiner, *Vorstufen zum Mysterium von Golgatha*, p. 46.

53 Ibid., p. 48.

54 Rudolf Steiner, *Mitteleuropa zwischen Ost und West.* CW 174a. Dornach 1982, p. 40.

55 *"It is Michael's task to lead human beings on the paths of the will to the place from whence we came, since we have descended with our earth consciousness on the paths of the will from the experience of the supersensory world to the experience of the sensory one"* (Rudolf Steiner. *Anthroposophische Leitsätze.* CW 26, p. 81). In regard to further Michaelic and Christological dimensions of the first part of the Warmth Meditation (preparation), see in particular Steiner's further maxims (in CW 26, pp. 114ff.) on the "love of action" as well as the boundedness of the spiritual will to the world. ("*When the human being seeks freedom without an impulse toward egoism, when freedom becomes a pure love for the capacity to act, then there is the possibility of drawing near to Michael.... Human beings become ever more human insofar as they become an expression of the world; I find myself, insofar as I do not seek myself, but bind myself willingly to the world in love*" Ibid., p. 117).

56 See also the lectures and remarks in Rudolf Steiner, *Geistige Wirkenskräfte im Zusammenleben von alter und junger Generation. Pädagogischer Jugendkurs.* CW 217 [E: *Becoming the Archangel Michael's Companions: Rudolf Steiner's Challenge to the Younger Generation* (Great Barrington, MA: SteinerBooks, 2006)]; and *Die Erkenntnis-Aufgabe der Jugend.* CW 217a [E: *Youth and the Etheric Heart: Rudolf Steiner Speaks to the Younger Generation* (Great Barrington, MA: SteinerBooks, 2007)]; my symptomalogical study of the early years of anthroposophical therapeutic pedagogy and the biographical, constellational forces in the young lives of its early personalities: *Der Engel über dem Lauenstein. Siegfried Pickerts Weg zu Rudolf Steiner und Ita Wegman.* In *Der Engel über dem Lauenstein. Siegfried Pickert, Ita Wegman und die Heilpädagogik.* Dornach 2004; as well as the relevant aspects of the great biographical works by Hermann Girke and Hans Müller-Wiedemann about Frank Löffler and Karl König (*Franz Löffler. Ein Leben für Anthroposophie und heilende Erziehung im Zeitenschicksal.* Dornach 1995; *Karl König. Eine mitteleuropäische Biogaphie im 20. Jahrhunder.* Stuttgart 1992).

57 Rudolf Steiner. *Eine okkulte Physiologie.* CW 128. Dornach 1991, p. 176. [E: *An Occult Physiology* (London: Rudolf Steiner Press, 1997)].

58 Peter Selg. *Helene von Grunelius*, pp. 31f.

59 Rudolf Steiner. *Die Brücke zwischen der Weltgeistigkeit und dem Physischen des Menschen*, pp. 170f.

60 See also Peter Selg. *Vom Logos menschlicher Physis. Die Enifaltung einer anthroposophischen Humanphysiologie im Werk Rudolf Steiners.* Dornach 2000, pp. 481ff.

61 Rudolf Steiner, *Die Brücke zwischen der Weltgeistigkeit und dem Physischen des Menschen*, p. 187.

62 Ibid.

63 Ibid., p. 189.

64 Peter Selg. *Helene von Grunelius*, p. 50.

65 Rudolf Steiner. *Esoterische Unterweisungen für die erste Klasse der Freien Hochschule für Geisteswissenschaft am Goetheanum 1924*. CW 270. Band II. p. 121.

66 Ibid., Band I, p. 105.

67 See Steiner's cosmogenetic remarks on *"old Saturn"* in the *Outline of Esoteric Science* (CW 13) as well as the descriptions in the Düsseldorf lecture cycle *Die geistigen Hierarchien und ihre Widerspiegelung in der physischen Welt*, in which he says, "*On this old Saturn, the first version of the physical human being was formed. In this very first form, it was actually formed out of warmth, but even in this warmth body, the seeds of all the later organs were already laid out. At the point where the first [Warmth] movement was excited and then came to rest, the position within the human body of that organ was established that then later, when it ceased its motion, also brought the entire motor of the physical body to rest—that is, the heart. Here, from that very first excitation of motion, the position of the heart was established, but this first position was only established because it was at this same point that the motion was also brought to rest. Because of that, the heart became that organ through which all the functions of the entire physical body could be brought to rest when it ceased its beating.*" (CW 110, Dornach 1972, p. 130. [E: *The Spiritual Hierarchies and the Physical World: Zodiac, Planets & Cosmos* (Great Barrington, MA: SteinerBooks, 2008)]). For the collective dimension of this theme, see also Peter Selg, *Mysterium cordis*. Dornach 2003, pp. 110ff. [E: *The Mystery of the Heart: The Sacramental Physiology of the Heart in Aristotle, Thomas Aqinas, and Rudolf Steiner* (Great Barrington, MA: SteinerBooks, 2012)].

68 Rudolf Steiner. *Esoterische Unterweisungen für die erste Klasse der Freien Hochschule für Geisteswissenschaft am Goetheanum 1924*. CW 270. Band II. p. 85.

69 Ibid., p. 93.

70 Rudolf Steiner. *Menschenwerden, Weltenseele und Weltengeist. Erster Teil*. CW 205. Dornach 1987, p. 111.

71 See Peter Selg, *Mysterium cordis*, pp. 126ff. [E: *The Mystery of the Heart: The Sacramental Physiology of the Heart in Aristotle, Thomas Aquinas, and Rudolf Steiner* (Great Barrington, MA: SteinerBooks, 2012)].

72 Rudolf Steiner, *Vorträge und Kurse uber christlich-religioses Wirken II*. CW 343. Dornach 1993, p. 427.

73 See also Peter Selg. *Krankheit, Heilung und Schicksal des Menschen. Über Rudolf Steiners geisteswissenschaftliches Pathologie- und Therapieverständnis*. Dornach 2004, pp. 109ff.

74 Rudolf Steiner, *Das esoterische Christentum und die geistige Führung der Menschheit*. CW 130. Dornach 1995, p. 174. [E: *Esoteric Christianity and the Mission of Christian Rosenkreutz* (London: Rudolf Steiner Press, 2001)]. See also Rudolf Steiner's further remarks in the cited Christological lecture delievered in Nuremberg on 12/2/1911.

75 See in particular the wide-reaching remarks in the Kassel lectures from June 5 and 6, 1909 (Rudolf Steiner, *Das Johannes-Evangelium im Verhältnis zu den drei anderen Evangelien, besonders zu dem Lukas-Evangelium*. CW 112. [E: *The Gospel of St. John and Its Relation to the Other Gospels* (Spring Valley, NY: Anthroposophic Press, 1982)]), in which Rudolf Steiner described successive possible "immersions" into the Christ-impulse in the human etheric body since the Mystery of Golgotha, and made his audiences aware of the preconditions for that sort of development (in the sense of a necessary Christ-relationship and

Christ-knowledge), as well as the constitutional results on the collective organism of the human being (leading toward an overcoming of luciferic and ahrimanic sicknesses within the physical body).

76 Rudolf Steiner. *Die okkulte Bewegung im neunzehnten Jahrhundert und ihre Beziehung zur Weltkultur.* CW 254. Dornach 1986, p. 109.

77 Rudolf Steiner. *Der Christus-Impuls und die Entwickelung des Ich-Bewusstseins.* CW 116. Dornach 1982, p. 93. See also Rudolf Steiner's remarks in Basel on 10/1/1911, according to which the union of the etheric bloodstream in the human being (from the heart to head) with the etheric earthly-cosmic blood stream of the Christ Jesus is the necessary precondition for the perception of the Christ in the etheric (in Rudolf Steiner, *Das estoerische Christentum und die geistige Führung der Welt.* CW 130). [E: *Esoteric Christianity and the Mission of Christian Rosenkreutz* (London: Rudolf Steiner Press, 2001)].

78 "How can...the human being prepare itself nowadays for beholding the Christ? In addition to other exercises, Rudolf Steiner indicates that one should learn to perceive the idea of the Good as a magical impulse, a task that is to be realized in the coming 3,000 years. How can a moral impulse become an organ of perception? If a moral ideal lives strongly enough within the soul, a soul warmth develops there, and in addition, a physical-etheric warmth is excited. From this, new sources of light, sound, and life come into being. Warmth, light, sound, and life: the four forms of our etheric body are activated. This allows the etheric body to take on a life of its own and allows it to become an 'organ' that learns naturally to look into its etheric surroundings" (Madeleine van Deventer, "*The reality in which we live.*" In *Das Goetheanum, Nachrichtenblatt Nr. 48.* 11/26/1972, p. 201).

79 Rudolf Steiner. *Das Lukas-Evangelium.* CW 114. Dornach 1985, p. 148. [E: *According to Luke: The Gospel of Compassion and Love Revealed* (Great Barrington, MA: SteinerBooks, 2001)].

80 Rudolf Steiner. *Esoterische Unterweisungen fur die erste Klasse der Freien Hochschule fur Geisteswissenschaft am Goetheanum 1924.* CW 270. Band I, p. 138.

81 *"What is it which makes everything that lives in our moral ideas effective in reality? It is the Christ—it is the Christ!"* (Rudolf Steiner, *Bausteine zu einer Erkenntnis des Mysteriums von Golgatha.* CW 175. Dornach 1982, p. 225 [E: *Building Stones for an Understanding of the Mystery of Golgotha: Human Life in a Cosmic Context* (London: Rudolf Steiner Press, 2015)]). See also Rudolf Steiner's remarks in Munich from Nov. 18, 1911, according to which the perception of the etheric Christ is connected with the achievement of the *"highest possible moral impulses"* for humanity. (Rudolf Steiner, *Das esoterische Christentum und die geistige Führung der Welt.* CW 130. Dornach 1995, p. 149). [E: *Esoteric Christianity and the Mission of Christian Rosenkreutz* (London: Rudolf Steiner Press, 2001)].

Books in English Translation by Peter Selg

On Rudolf Steiner

Rudolf Steiner: Life and Work: *(1914–1918): The Years of World War I* , vol. 4 of 7 (2016)

Rudolf Steiner: Life and Work: *(1900–1914): Spiritual Science and Spiritual Community*, vol. 3 of 7 (2015)

Rudolf Steiner: Life and Work: *(1890–1900): Weimar and Berlin*, vol. 2 of 7 (2014)

Rudolf Steiner: Life and Work: *(1861–1890): Childhood, Youth, and Study Years*, vol. 1 of 7 (2014)

Rudolf Steiner and Christian Rosenkreutz (2012)

Rudolf Steiner as a Spiritual Teacher: *From Recollections of Those Who Knew Him* (2010)

On Christology

The Sufferings of the Nathan Soul: *Anthroposophic Christology on the Eve of World War I* (2016)

The Lord's Prayer and Rudolf Steiner: *A Study of His Insights into the Archetypal Prayer of Christianity* (2014)

The Creative Power of Anthroposophical Christology: *An Outline of Occult Science · The First Goetheanum · The Fifth Gospel · The Christmas Conference* (with Sergei O. Prokofieff) (2012)

Christ and the Disciples: *The Destiny of an Inner Community* (2012)

The Figure of Christ: *Rudolf Steiner and the Spiritual Intention behind the Goetheanum's Central Work of Art* (2009)

Rudolf Steiner and the Fifth Gospel: *Insights into a New Understanding of the Christ Mystery* (2010)

Seeing Christ in Sickness and Healing (2005)

ON GENERAL ANTHROPOSOPHY

The Warmth Meditation: *Historical Background and Spiritual Connections* (2016)

The Destiny of the Michael Community: *Foundation Stone for the Future* (2014)

Spiritual Resistance: *Ita Wegman 1933–1935* (2014)

The Last Three Years: *Ita Wegman in Ascona, 1940–1943* (2014)

From Gurs to Auschwitz: *The Inner Journey of Maria Krehbiel-Darmstädter* (2013)

Crisis in the Anthroposophical Society: *And Pathways to the Future* (2013); with Sergei O. Prokofieff

Rudolf Steiner's Foundation Stone Meditation: *And the Destruction of the Twentieth Century* (2013)

The Culture of Selflessness: *Rudolf Steiner, the Fifth Gospel, and the Time of Extremes* (2012)

The Mystery of the Heart: *The Sacramental Physiology of the Heart in Aristotle, Thomas Aquinas, and Rudolf Steiner* (2012)

Rudolf Steiner and the School for Spiritual Science: *The Foundation of the "First Class"* (2012)

Rudolf Steiner's Intentions for the Anthroposophical Society: *The Executive Council, the School for Spiritual Science, and the Sections* (2011)

The Fundamental Social Law: *Rudolf Steiner on the Work of the Individual and the Spirit of Community* (2011)

The Path of the Soul after Death: *The Community of the Living and the Dead as Witnessed by Rudolf Steiner in his Eulogies and Farewell Addresses* (2011)

The Agriculture Course, Koberwitz, Whitsun 1924: *Rudolf Steiner and the Beginnings of Biodynamics* (2010)

On Anthroposophical Medicine and Curative Education

Honoring Life: *Medical Ethics and Physician-Assisted Suicide* (2014); with Sergei O. Prokofieff

I Am for Going Ahead: *Ita Wegman's Work for the Social Ideals of Anthroposophy* (2012)

The Child with Special Needs: *Letters and Essays on Curative Education* (Ed.) (2009)

Ita Wegman and Karl König: *Letters and Documents* (2008)

Karl König's Path to Anthroposophy (2008)

Karl König: My Task: *Autobiography and Biographies* (Ed.) (2008)

On Child Development and Waldorf Education

I Am Different from You: *How Children Experience Themselves and the World in the Middle of Childhood* (2011)

Unbornness: *Human Pre-existence and the Journey toward Birth* (2010)

The Essence of Waldorf Education (2010)

The Therapeutic Eye: *How Rudolf Steiner Observed Children* (2008)

A Grand Metamorphosis: *Contributions to the Spiritual-Scientific Anthropology and Education of Adolescents* (2008)

Ita Wegman Institute
for Basic Research into Anthroposophy

Pfeffinger Weg 1a, ch 4144 Arlesheim, Switzerland
www.wegmaninstitut.ch
e-mail: sekretariat@wegmaninstitut.ch

The Ita Wegman Institute for Basic Research into Anthroposophy is a non-profit research and teaching organization. It undertakes basic research into the lifework of Dr. Rudolf Steiner (1861–1925) and the application of Anthroposophy in specific areas of life, especially medicine, education, and curative education. Work carried out by the Institute is supported by a number of foundations and organizations and an international group of friends and supporters. The Director of the Institute is Prof. Dr. Peter Selg.